SCHAUM SOLO PIANO ALBUMS FOR THE YOUNG STUDENT

THE CHRISTMAS BOOK

Arrangements by John W. Schaum and Wesley Schaum

CONTENTS

Editors: David C. Olsen and Carole Flatau

LET IT SNOW! LET IT SNOW! LET IT SNOW!

Lyric by
SAMMY CAHN

Music by JULE STYNE
Arranged by WESLEY SCHAUM

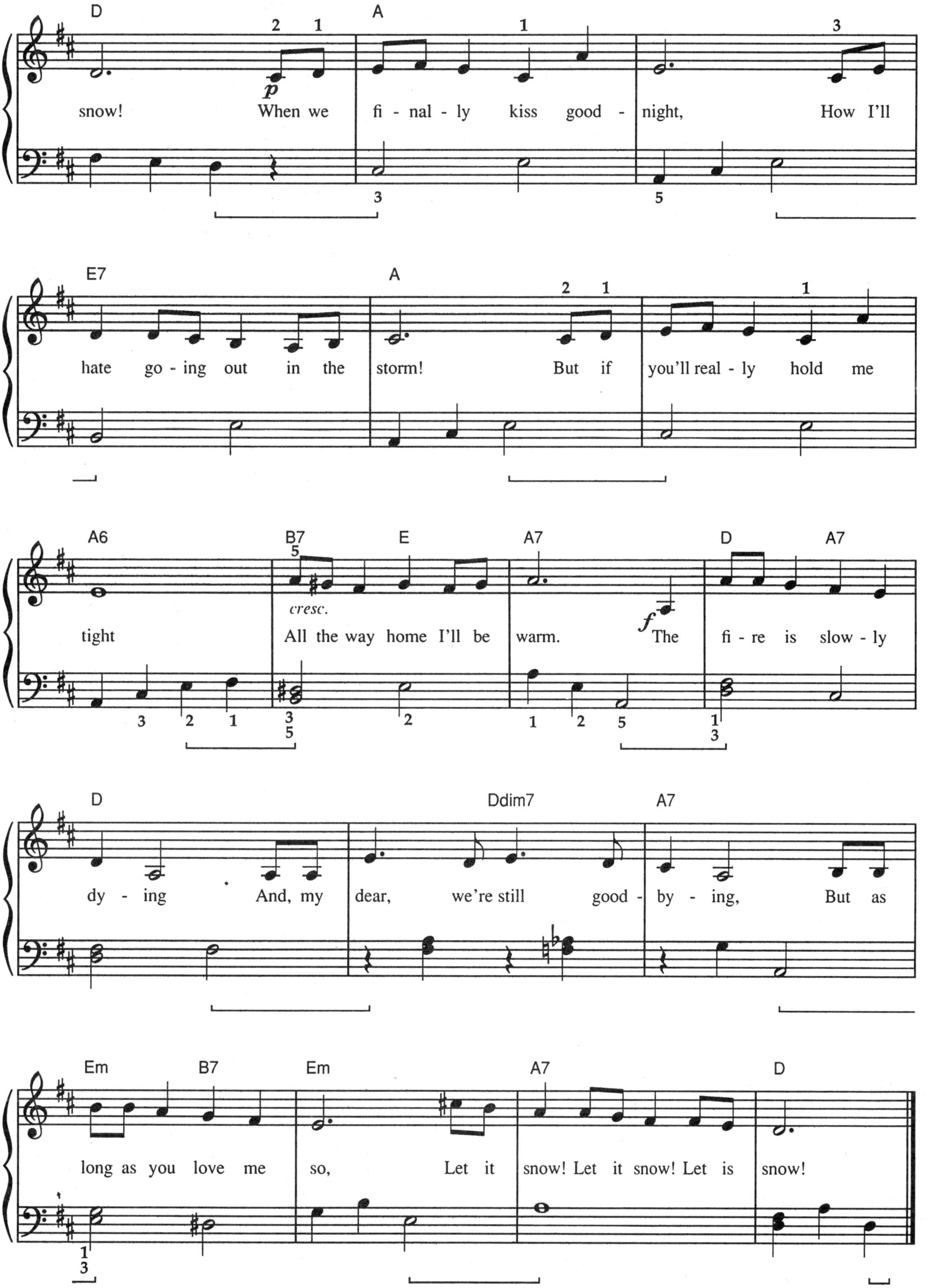
D A E7 A A6 B7 E A7 D A7 D Ddim7 A7 Em B7 Em A7 D
snow! When we fi - nal - ly kiss good - night, How I'll
hate go - ing out in the storm! But if you'll real - ly hold me
tight All the way home I'll be warm. The fi - re is slow - ly
dy - ing And, my dear, we're still good - by - ing, But as
long as you love me so, Let it snow! Let it snow! Let is snow!
cresc.

Rudolph, the Red-Nosed Reindeer

by Johnny Marks
arr. by John W. Schaum

Giocoso

F C Dm G7 C C♯dim
mf
Then one fog - gy Christ-mas Eve, San - ta came to say
G G♯dim Am D7 G7
"Ru-dolph with your nose so bright, won't you guide my sleigh to-night?"
C E♭dim G7
f
Then how the rein-deer loved him as they shout-ed out with glee.
C
"Ru-dolph, the red-nosed rein-deer, you'll go down in his - to - ry!"

Little Drummer Boy

Words and Music by
Davis, Onorati, Simeone
arr. by John W. Schaum

Marcato

C F
p
rum pum pum pum, So to hon - or Him pa
C F
rum pum pum pum, when we come,
C F7 B♭ F
cresc. f dim.
I played my best for Him, pa - rum pum pum pum, rum pum pum pum,
C F
p
rum pum pum pum, Then He smiled at me pa -
C F
rum pum pum pum, me and my drum.

Santa Claus Is Comin' to Town

Words by Haven Gillespie

Music by J. Fred Coots

arr. by Wesley Schaum

Moderato

C7 F C7 F
sees you when you're sleep - in' he knows when you're a - wake, he
D7 G D7 G7
knows if you've been bad or good, so be good for good-ness sake. Oh! you
mf
C F C
bet - ter watch out, you bet - ter not cry, bet - ter not pout, I'm
F C Am Dm G7 C6
tell-ing you why: San - ta Claus is com - in' to town.

Have Yourself a Merry Little Christmas

Words and Music by
Hugh Martin and Ralph Blane
arr. by Wesley Schaum

Moderato

F C G7 CM7
Here we are as in old-en days, hap-py gold-en days of yore.
Am6 Em D7 G7
Faith-ful friends who are dear to us gath-er near to us once more.
C G7 C G7
Through the years we all will be to-geth-er, if the fates al-low.
C E7 Am C7
Hang a shin-ing star up-on the high-est bough. And
F G7 C6
have your-self a mer-ry lit-tle Christ-mas now.

Sleigh Ride

Words by Mitchell Parish

Music by Leroy Anderson

arr. by Wesley Schaum

A6 Bm7 E7 AM7 A6
show, We're rid-ing in a won-der-land of snow. Gid-dy-
Am7 D7 GM7 G6
yap, gid-dy-yap, gid-dy-yap, it's grand, Just hold-ing your hand.
Gm7 C7 Gm7 C7 C+
We're glid-ing a-long with a song of a win-ter-y fair-y-land. Our cheeks are
F C7 F6 C7
nice and ros-y, and com-fy co-zy are we; We're snug-gled
F C7 F6
up to-geth-er like two birds of a feath-er would be. Let's take that

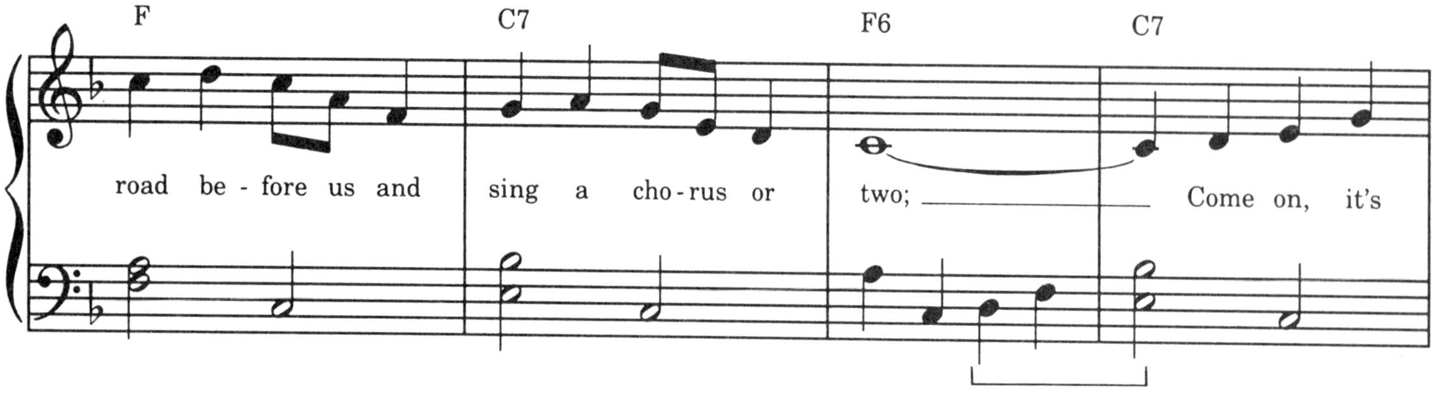

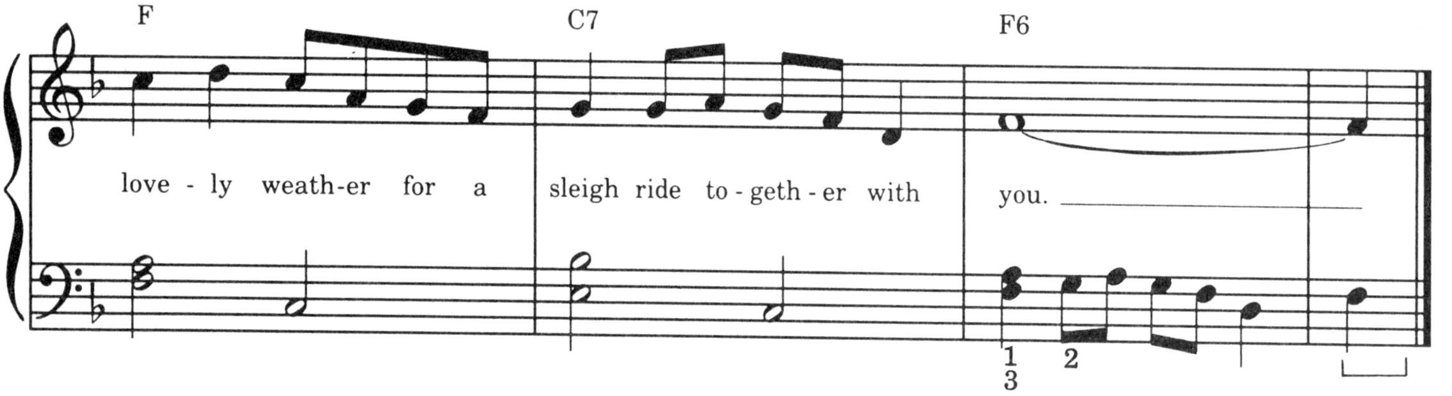

I'll Be Home for Christmas

Lyric by Kim Gannon

Music by Walter Kent
arr. by Wesley Schaum

Andantino

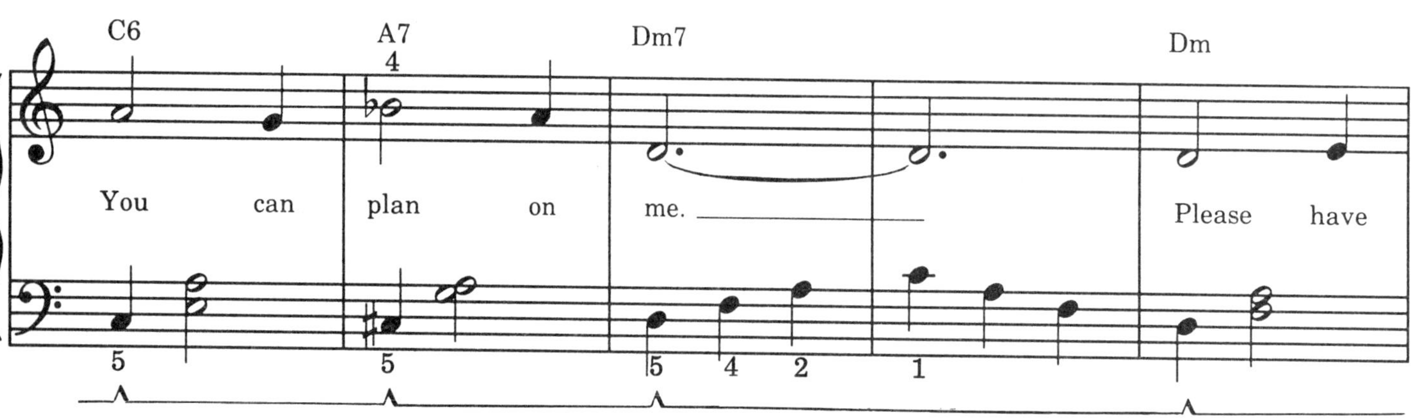

Fm6 C Am Am7
snow and mis - tle - toe and pre - sents
D7 Dm G7 C
on the tree. Christ - mas Eve will
C6 A7
find me Where the love - light
Dm7 F Fm Em7-5
gleams, I'll be home for Christ -
A7 Dm G7 F C
mas, if on - ly in my dreams.

I Saw Mommy Kissing Santa Claus

Words and Music by
Tommie Connor
arr. by Wesley Schaum

C6 Em7
I saw Mom - my tick - le San - ta Claus,
C6 C7 F6
Un - der neath his beard so snow - y white;
Oh, what a
B7 C6 G7
laugh it would have been, If Dad - dy had on - ly seen Mom - my
C6 Dm7-5 G7 C6
kiss - ing San - ta Claus last night.

Gesu Bambino

Words by Frederick H. Martens
Music by Pietro A. Yon
arr. by John W. Schaum

Cantabile

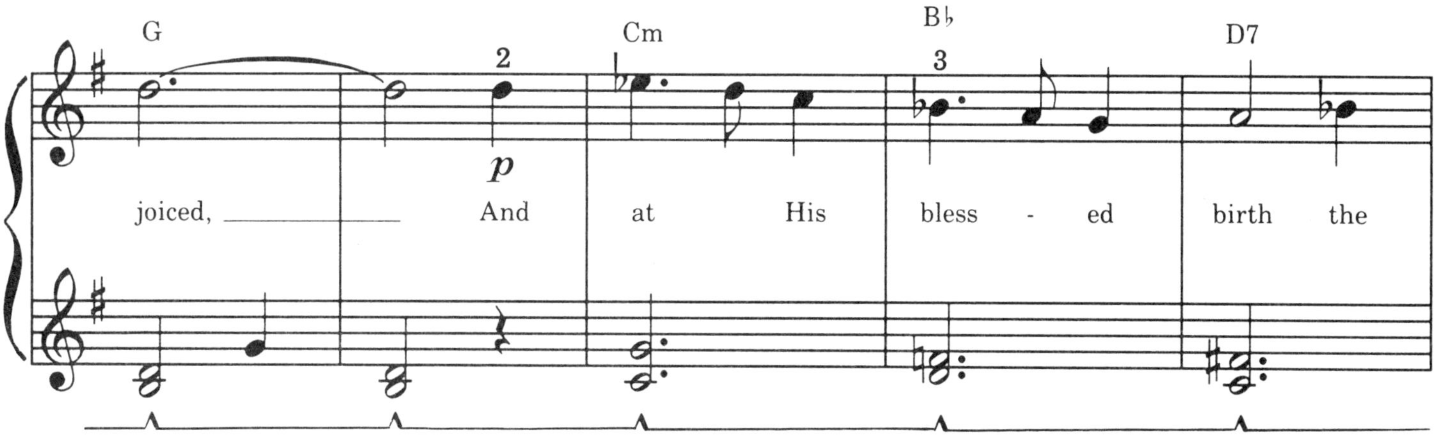

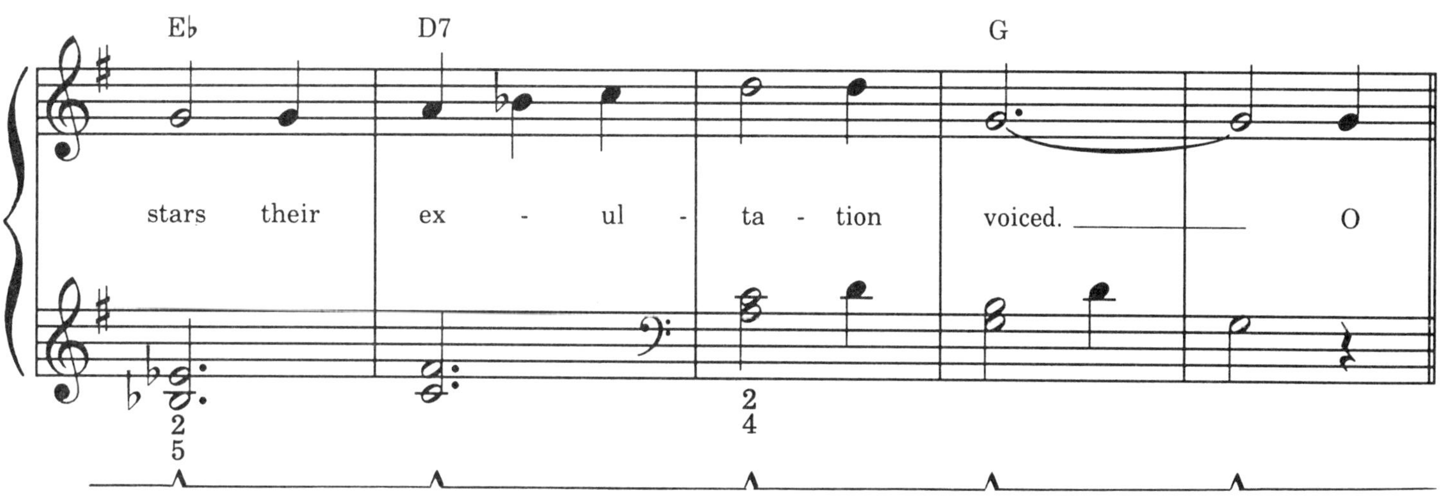

Note: Another person may play the duet accompaniment part in combination with the main theme.

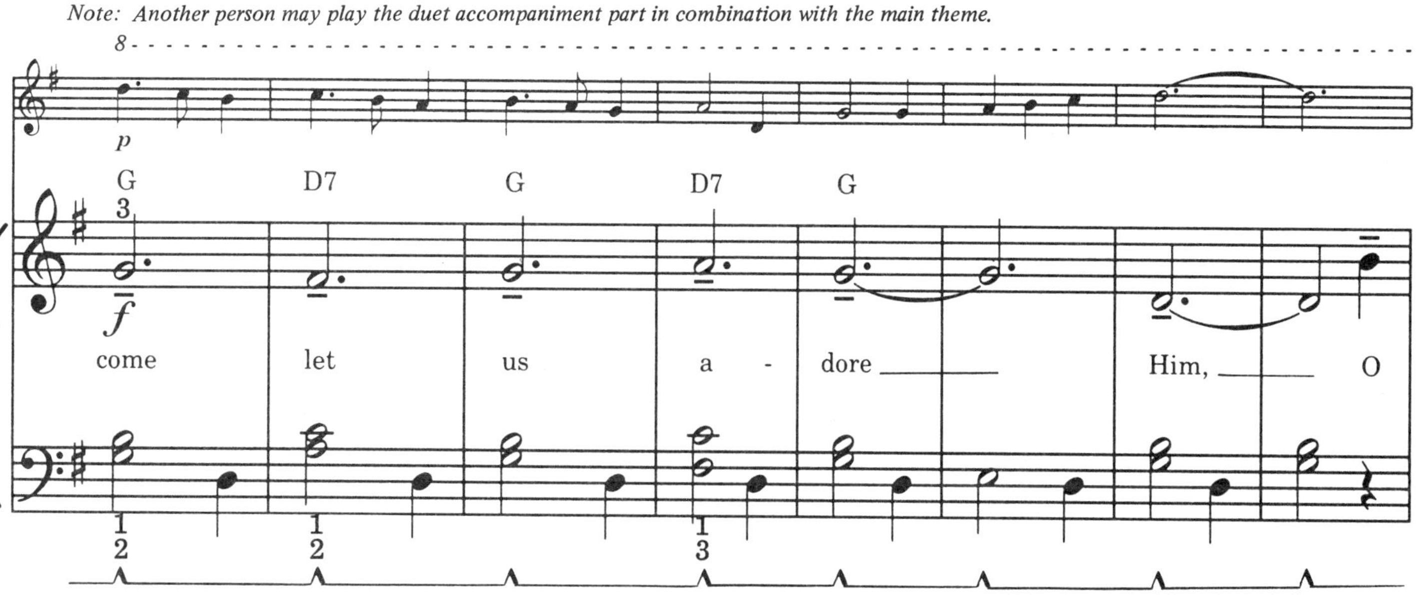

D7 G C G D7
come let us a - dore Him, O
C G C G D7 G C
come let us a - dore Him
G D7 G
Christ the Lord

Here Comes Santa Claus

(Right Down Santa Claus Lane)

Words and Music by
Gene Autry and Oakley Haldeman
arr. by Wesley Schaum

A Holly Jolly Christmas

By Johnny Marks
arr. by Wesley Schaum

Allegretto

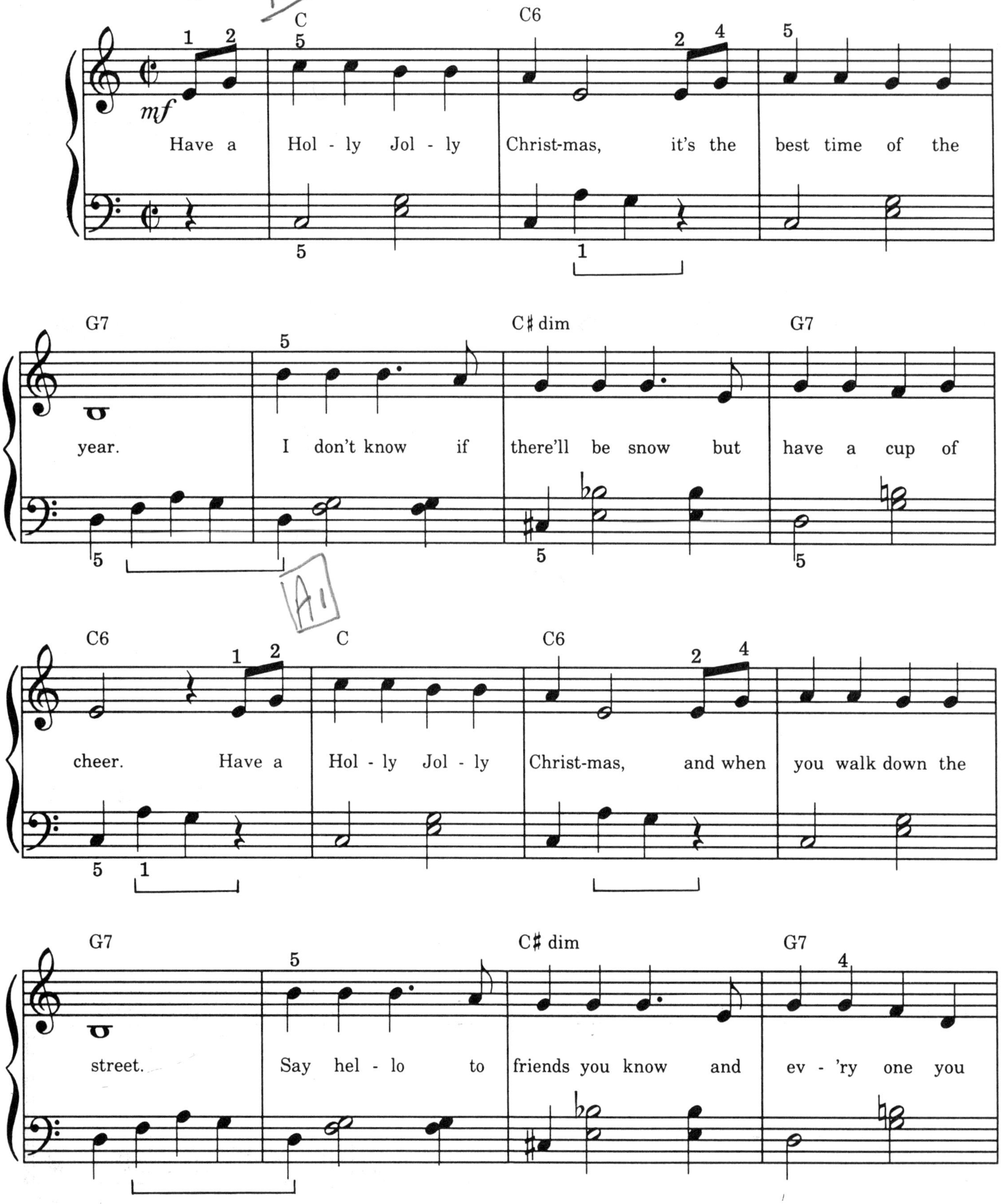

C6 F Em F
meet. Oh, ho, the mis - tle - toe hung where you can
C6 Dm Am D7
see. Some - bod - y waits for you, kiss her once for
G7 C C6 C
me. Have a hol - ly jol - ly Christ-mas, and in case you did - n't
G7 C G7 C
hear. Oh, by gol-ly, have a hol - ly jol - ly Christ-mas this year.

WESLEY SCHAUM

As a composer, editor, publisher, and clinician, Wesley Schaum has written, arranged, and edited more than 170 books and sheet music pieces for piano, organ, and keyboard teaching since 1959. He has presented numerous workshops to teacher groups across the United States. His music is available in special editions distributed in England, Germany, and Holland.

Mr. Schaum began piano study at the age of five with his mother and continued lessons with his father, John W. Schaum. Wesley started private teaching at the age of fifteen and continued teaching while attending college. While serving in the Navy, he was a piano instructor and registrar of the U.S. Navy School of Music and served as chapel organist. He is currently director of the Schaum Music School in Mequon, Wisconsin, with an enrollment of more than 200 students each week.

A member of two honorary fraternities, Mr. Schaum was an honors graduate and soloist with the university band and orchestra at Northwestern University where he earned bachelor of music and master of music degrees.

Recently, in collaboration with editors at Warner Bros. Publications, Mr. Schaum assisted in the revision of his father's *Schaum Piano Course, Schaum Note Spellers, Schaum Theory Lessons, Harmony Lessons,* and other Schaum supplementary books.

JOHN W. SCHAUM

Founder and director of the Schaum Music School in Milwaukee, Wisconsin, John W. Schaum is the composer of internationally famous piano teaching materials including more than 200 books and 450 sheet music pieces. He is author of the internationally acclaimed *Schaum Piano Course* published by Belwin-Mills Publishing Corporation/Warner Bros. Publications. During his extensive travels, Mr. Schaum presented hundreds of piano teacher workshops in all fifty states. He was president of the Wisconsin Music Teachers Association and soloist with the Milwaukee Philharmonic Orchestra.

Mr. Schaum received a master of music degree from Northwestern University, a bachelor of music degree from Marquette University, and a bachelor of music education degree from the University of Wisconsin-Milwaukee.

He remains an important influence in the lives of hundreds of thousands of piano students who have enjoyed and continue to play his music.